PRAISE FOR common grace: *poems*

"The quality of wonder, lucid and luminous, energizes Aaron Caycedo-Kimura's *Common Grace*. In these poems, the visible world radiates meaning, memory becomes palpable, and loss is acknowledged. Caycedo-Kimura brings a wry, tender, musical and unsentimental attention to family love, sexual love, love of nature and the underlying love of art."

—Robert Pinsky, three-time United States Poet Laureate

"These well-wrought poems show a distinct artistic sensibility. Through personal loss, grief, and love, they enter the domain of history and human migrations. *Common Grace* is an uncommon book, elegant, at times tough-minded, also moving."

—Ha Jin, National Book Award–winning author of *Waiting*

"I love the tender, lyrical '*labored stroke*' with which poet-painter Aaron Caycedo-Kimura makes his art. With a poet's sensibility and an artist's cool eye, he elegizes and celebrates his family's heartbreaking, triumphant history, and his own. *Common Grace*, his first full-length collection, pays fluent loving attention to life and art—and their rewards glow!"

—Gail Mazur, author of *Land's End: New and Selected Poems*

T0025749

"In vivid, moving poems that span cultures, generations, and geographies, Aaron Caycedo-Kimura's *Common Grace* evokes the mysteries and wonder in everyday life. Here is a poet of clear-eyed originality, big-hearted and wise—and a book to read again and again."

—Matthew Thorburn, author of *The Grace of Distance*

"*Common Grace* (with its striking images, chorus of different forms, and historical narratives, including those of Japanese internment) announces Caycedo-Kimura as an important new voice making art from the complexities and contradictions of being a third-generation Japanese American. . . . The poems in *Common Grace* offer us both beauty and wisdom in equal measure."

—Jennifer Franklin, author of *No Small Gift*

common grace

Also by Aaron Caycedo-Kimura

Ubasute

Text, Don't Call:
An Illustrated Guide to the Introverted Life

common grace

Poems

AARON CAYCEDO-KIMURA

Raised Voices   BEACON PRESS   Boston

BEACON PRESS
Boston, Massachusetts
www.beacon.org

Beacon Press books
are published under the auspices of
the Unitarian Universalist Association of Congregations.

Raised Voices: a poetry series established in 2021 to raise marginalized
voices and perspectives, to publish poems that affirm progressive values
and are accessible to a wide readership, and to celebrate poetry's ability
to access truth in a way that no other form can.

25 24 23 22   8 7 6 5 4 3 2 1

This book is printed on acid-free paper that meets the uncoated paper
ANSI/NISO specifications for permanence as revised in 1992.

Text design by Michael Starkman
at Wilsted & Taylor Publishing Services

LIBRARY OF CONGRESS CATALOGING-IN-PUBLICATION DATA
Names: Caycedo-Kimura, Aaron T., author.
Title: Common grace : poems / Aaron Caycedo-Kimura.
Other titles: Common grace (Compilation)
Description: Boston : Beacon Press, [2022] | Summary: "A poetry collection
    exploring the author's personal life, the passing of his parents, and his
    close relationship with his wife"—Provided by publisher.
Identifiers: LCCN 2022019774 | ISBN 9780807015889 (paperback) |
    ISBN 9780807015902 (ebook)
Subjects: LCGFT: Poetry.
Classification: LCC PS3603.A978 C66 2022 | DDC 813/.6—dc23/
    eng/20220607
LC record available at https://lccn.loc.gov/2022019774

To Luisa
and the memory of my parents

CONTENTS

I. Soul Sauce

II. Ubasute

III. Gutter Trees

I. Soul Sauce

Family Anthem

I walk into the garage   from side door sunlight
ELO on my Walkman   my eyes dissolve   the darkness
discover my parents   locked   in a slow-dance
embrace   whispering to each other   like lovers

but my parents aren't lovers   they're Japanese   never kiss
hold hands   say *I love you*   not even to me
once I asked Mom   if she loved me   she replied
my mother and father   never said it   but I knew they did

my parents hear my shuffle   separate like guilty teenagers
she escapes   into the house   he into the Ford   opens
the garage door   I fumble   forget what I was looking for
but all afternoon   replay   that dissonant chord

Chopsticks

I open the oven to check
the fries—waft of potato,
a puff of steam fogs

my glasses. Not thinking,
I pick one up. Too hot.
It drops into the crack

where the door hinges
on the oven. *Ohashi!*
Ohashi! I scream to Luisa,

who gives me that *who are you*
and what have you done
with my husband? look.

How did this word erupt
from my mouth? I haven't used
it in years—only as a boy

in my home where Mom
did her best to teach me
some Japanese and I grew

4

reluctant to learn. In panic,
unable to offer translation,
I reach for the chopsticks

on the counter. And like playing
the game Operation, free
the fry from its slot.

Cal Tjader

Hypnagogic disks   rotating inside
the resonators   eight red mallets   bounce
off the alloy bars   plinging   plunking out
soul sauce   hot spun by a jade spider
throughout the Black Hawk club   on Turk and Hyde
clinging   to every eardrum in the crowd
congas   timbales   guiro   and cowbell
bossa nova and mambo   hypnotize

Ken Williams   at Drumland on Ellis
years ago   loaned me a Deagan   once owned
by Cal   it didn't help this web-stuck bug
when Cal plays   I want to drive   down Route 1
to Monterey   dive   into the ocean
Afro Blue   *Linda Chicana*   *Soul Sauce*

titling a poem

all afternoon   a fly buzzes   bumps against glass

En Plein Air at Silver Sands State Park

I block in the lights and darks of a cottonwood grove
that looks like a moldy muffin floating on my canvas.
The flies and wetland whiff of rotten egg will keep me
from staying much longer. As I use the last dab of sap green
on my palette, a woman walking a black Lab stops to look.
She tilts her head, nods. *Do you remember Bob Ross?*
She loved his "happy trees," how he made them so easy
with the edge of his brush. She yanks her dog from sniffing
my easel's leg—*C'mon boy*—leaves me to my landscape.
I end up staying all morning, struggling with my trees,
trying to make art with each labored stroke.

Winter Psalm

O LORD, strip me like the sycamore
    in winter, white bark branches
        stretched out in surrender.

It makes no effort to hide
    it's not as enduring as the mountains
        or prudish like the spruce and pine.

Today I walked down South Main,
    passed a man going the other way.
        We said nothing, didn't even look up.

Bundled in gray jackets, hunched over,
    hands stuffed in pockets, we pretended
        to be protecting ourselves from the cold.

Roseland Elementary, 1969

You get your hand stuck in the inkwell
hole of your desk—that's what happens
when you're bored. Miss Freeman yanks

it out hard like a deformed turnip
plucked from the dirt. She shakes it
in your face. *Look how red that is!*

When the bell rings, the other kids run
to the playground; you walk to a bench,
the one with peeling green paint.

In her blue sailor dress and knee-high socks
Denise yells from the tetherball,
Hey Ching-Chong, come here!
Her short blonde hair, almost white.

You're the only Japanese kid at Roseland.
Every night you tell your mother, *I don't*
want to go to school anymore. She says,
We all have to do things we don't want to.

You walk to the tetherball—maybe Denise
likes you? She serves the ball with both hands.
It flies above your head, then back down around.
She smacks the ball faster and faster

until the winding rope chokes the pole.
The fall wind smells like wet sawdust,
blows dead oak leaves across the blacktop.
You imagine jumping into a well of ink.

Sunflowers

Last to arrive, they tower
eight feet in the garden
like reapers come to survey

their work. They bow
their monocular heads,
giving thanks for today's

rain. As the air crisps
and the sun zippers across
the sky, they lead us

into harvest, goldfinches
pecking out their eyes.

Elegy for Mrs. Mullane

You pointed to a quartz-colored vase on a shelf in the pottery shop. *See how they made that?* you said to us with your slight southern accent. It was constructed of quadrilateral patches of clay—oval mouth, jagged lip. *You can make that, too!* I only knew you for a couple of months, took your ceramics class in a summer program between sixth and seventh grades. I didn't make that vase, but fashioned a pot by what you called the ring method—rings of clay stacked one upon the other, held together by scoring and slip. You glazed it for me, dipped the top in white. I decorated it with linked Cs painted in iron oxide. Forty-five years later, it sits here in my art studio, where I sit, studying paintings and poems to see how they were made.

In the Studio

Arranged on a table behind my easel—
a red sake bottle, blue glass vase,
an ochre bowl I bought for a dollar
at Goodwill. Joni Mitchell plays

on my laptop. I slosh a #5 flat brush
in the wash container's cloudy turp,
let it soak in the strainer, step away
from the canvas five or six feet.

Bowl's too flat. Some lighter touches
in front will round it out. The background's
kind of warm. A few strokes of blue-gray
should cool it down, push it back.

Joni sings "California." After flying back
to Santa Rosa when my father died,
I returned home, met Tineka for coffee.
She'd show my work if I didn't drip

and spatter. For a while, I painted
to please her. Then canceled my show,
let my brushes harden, my palette crust.

Back at the easel, I grab a tube
of ultramarine, squeeze a dab
on my palette. Slather in some
vermillion, ochre, titanium white.

Joni takes me back to junior high.
I'd lose myself in study hall, scribbling
and sketching all over the book covers
I made from brown paper bags.

North on Route 101

For A.H.

She drives up the winding coast twenty miles
per hour in Pacific fog, like she's searching
for a line, alla prima, with the worn
bristles of a flat brush. In every twist,
she focuses on the road, not the drop-offs.
The fog dissipates—swatches of wild rye,
reedgrass, and sky spread across the windshield.

Back on the other coast—dishes, pots, pans,
a job. Most of her clothes. Tonight, she'll sleep
near the foot of Mount St. Helens, wake up
to a sun eruption of hansa yellow
and cadmium orange. She'll sketch a stream
tumbling toward her over a fallen cedar—
a sprinkling of pastel dust in her lap.

daily news

we all row the same boat   over falls

La Sidrería

The *escanciador* raises
the uncorked bottle
over his head,

throws a gulp
into the glass
held below his waist.

The stream aerates,
releases apple,
plunges into stars.

He hands the *culín*
of Asturias to a local
who stands at the bar

like the toothpicks
that pair bread and *queso*
on the tray to his left.

In one shot
he tosses it back,
leaves a little

to pour out
even though
there is no sediment.

Taxi de Toledo

Quixote's ghost charges his Peugeot
through ancient ravines, threads
his lance without flinching around corners
cut from the mountain. Like saints

in the cathedral's arches, Toledanos
on either side fade into doorways
before we pass—the street barely a lane,
a foot on each side of the bumper.

My driver has memorized every vein
in this rock like El Greco's brush
that licked muscle and bone
of the apostles' hands. Nowhere

to pull over, my driver halts with cars
behind, unloads my luggage.
With a cheerful *Va-le*, he gallops off—
Cervantes in his glove compartment.

Duende

at the Shark Bar on Amsterdam   my date and I sip
martinis   her eyes trance inward   untangle roots
reaching deep to a stone   she says she once grabbed

the hair   of her ex's rebound   twisted horse tail
liquid   around the veins of her fist   stretched
accordion wheeze   from the girl's neck

stirring her drink   with the cocktail stick
she sucks the olives   of my lidless eyes   cackles
a crashing breaker   vodka splashes   everywhere

Misfortuned

After Edward Hopper's *Chop Suey*, 1929

a man lights a cigarette   at the next table
my wool coat and scarf   hanging in the sun behind me
soak up the smell   of fried rice   garlic sauce   smoke

we've lingered   long enough   this November afternoon
talked about jobs   children   a failed marriage

before we get up   walk freeze-dried   New York streets
you lean in   read your fortune to me   again

under the clicking and clinking   silverware and dishes
you say   *I have your fortune*   *you got my life*

Turning Forty-Nine

Martini glass and tumbler commiserate
on my nightstand in an after-party
of ointments, Tums, and Tylenol.
One glass is dry, like scripted,
uninspired words. The toothpick
that speared gin-soaked olives
waits for disposal, chewed
and bent. The other glass pools
an amber drop, begs me to savor
the sip, as if it were the cure
to my depression. The weight
of my comforter traps my legs,
shackles me to the bed I've made,
unmade, made again—no wonder
I can't run far in my dreams.
In straitjacket rage, I fling
my covers to the floor only to realize
how ridiculous I look—body exposed,
aching, sagging. My head sinks
deep into the pillow, a confidant
swallowing drool and secrets,
as I fall asleep to a lullaby improv'd
by a polyphony of traffic and dogs.

Fishboned

The nurse asks *Have you had any surgeries?*
so I say, *I don't know if this counts, but* . . .
and tell her about the time I got a fish bone
stuck in my throat when I was five,
had to stay at the hospital overnight.
I mention the Donald Duck toilet seat—
thought it might bite—and Mom leaving
her cream-colored gloves inside the railing
of my bed. Or was that in a story
she read to me? The doctor who removed
the bone wore a head mirror. It looked
like a dish antenna on the lunar module.
Why would you feed a bony fish
to a five-year-old kid? I ask.
That's a question I should ask my parents—
or a shrink—but Mom and Dad
are gone. And I'm fifty-one.
Besides, it was only flounder.
The nurse types a few words on her laptop.
Probably "Loser. No surgeries."
I adjust my glutes, further crinkling
the paper on the examination table.
I want to think I've been wronged
somehow that I should be so awkward.

Cross My Heart, Hope to Die

My retina specialist says she's going to give me two injections in my left eyeball: the first with a very fine needle to numb the area and the second five minutes later with the medication. She doesn't comment on the thickness of the second needle, so I imagine one that's suitable for knitting a sweater. She tilts back the exam chair, pulls down my lower lid with her gloved fingers. The first shot stabs the glossy white of my eye. I feel the pinch. *Keep your eyes closed, and I'll be back in a few minutes*, she says. I pray the anesthetic will numb me before she returns. Five minutes later, she attaches a metal eyelid spreader to the edges of my socket à la Kubrick's *A Clockwork Orange*. I barely feel the shot, but she hits a vessel. My conjunctiva fills with blood around the iris. *It happens. I'm sorry*, my doctor says. *I'll see you in a month for a checkup.* As I check out at the front desk, dabbing rosé tears from my lids, there's a glass jar full of logoed plastic pens—retractable with triangular shafts that wedge snug in the nest of your fingers. Before walking out, I grab the handful I deserve.

Autumnal Equinox

Yesterday evening I walked up Beacon toward Commonwealth—not many people out. As if my presence caused it, all the streetlights blinked on at once. For a moment, I thought something else might happen: a chance encounter with a classmate, a twenty-dollar bill crumpled in the gutter, the perfect ending to a poem writing itself in autumn drizzle on the sidewalk. I stuffed my hands deeper into the pockets of my hoodie, continued my walk around Uno's and onto Boylston. The lights probably flicked off in a similar way at dawn when I was sleeping. I always thought I would like to be asleep when my lights go out. Completely unconscious like my Uncle Walter, whose heart disintegrated under a surgeon's scalpel. This morning walking to class down Bay State in the breeze—leaves shimmering, cheering me on—I realize it would be better to die laughing.

dying

unrehearsed   you walk onstage   only the dead clap

II. Ubasute

The Moon of Ubasute

After the woodblock
by Tsukioka Yoshitoshi

Years from now,
when I am old,
blind and crippled,
his mother said,
you must carry
me up the slope
of Tanigawa,
past the ancient
knotted pine,
leave me in a cradle
of hakone *grass*
and moss. Without pity,
my son, the moon
will watch as I reach
for my mother—
Okaasan, Okaasan.
The ginkgos will bow,
weep their leaves,
bury me in gold.

Burial

I returned my father's body to the earth
cremated as he instructed in a letter
no funeral no obituary in the newspaper
those who needed to know were told

I had his remains cremated as he instructed
scattered his ashes in Bodega Bay
those who needed to know were told
that I waited until my mother passed

to scatter his ashes in Bodega Bay
past the jetty where we used to fish
I waited until my mother passed
poured out their dust together

past the jetty where we used to fish
from the deck of the *Miss Anita* seagulls calling overhead
I poured out their dust together
with a handful of Uncle George

from the deck of the *Miss Anita* seagulls calling overhead
no funeral no obituary in the newspaper
with a handful of Uncle George
I returned their bodies to the earth

Hand Tilling

He chuffs his shovel   into soil   with the sole
of his right boot   more dried mud than leather

he balances full weight   both feet   on the shoulders
of the shovel   gloved hands rocking the handle   blade

prying packed clay   he levers a clod   turns it
hacks it   repeats down an eight-foot row   to his right

the smell of earth takes him back   to San Gabriel   the family
farm of rented acreage   before the War   before
Executive Order 9066   eviction   incarceration

after tilling four beds   he plants the shovel   upright
like a gnomon   marking time   rests on the pine bench

under the pin oak   he takes a swig from a can of Coors
surveys his garden   never needs to look   beyond his fence

Watching Grass Grow

Mari and I lie on our bellies—
tiny fists under tiny chins—staring
at a rectangle of dirt outlined
by pine stakes and kite string. Dad
has planted grass seed off the side
of the driveway, says if we're patient,
watch closely, we'll see it grow.

Mari whispers, *I don't see anything.*
Expecting some magic, I yell,
It's moving! but it's just an ant
crawling over boulders of soil.
We get up, dust ourselves off,
go inside to watch cartoons.

After April rain and sun, we have
a front lawn. Backyard, too.
Tricycles, swing set, swimming pool,
and bedrooms of our own. As we

get older, we wonder at how Dad
is so content with a tract home,
his glacier blue station wagon,
a small plot of land he waters
and grooms year after year.

His family owned just what they
could carry to Jerome and Tule Lake.
He never mentioned that. The only grass
he saw at the Santa Anita "Assembly Center"
was in the middle of the racetrack
near the horse stalls where his family slept.

Ride Home

Dad blows cigarette smoke
out the station wagon window.
It swirls back in, mixing
with the stink of seawater, perch,
and flounder. On a back road

home from Bodega Bay,
a morning of fishing off the jetty,
we drive with nothing much to say.
The vinyl seat hot under my thighs,
feet barely touching the floor,
the twisty road making me carsick.

He turns on the radio,
punches a buck-toothed button
for his favorite oldies station.
He fiddles with the knob
but can't get rid of the static

over Lena Horne. At Freestone
General Store, he buys two bottles
of Sprite. The bubbles scratch my throat,
but the cold sips of lemon-lime
give us something to talk about.

The *Miss Anita*

A fishing boat sails
past the jetty
heads toward the bay
like an angel
skimming water

her train of wave
and foam fans out
whips the breakwater
tide pools into
salty confetti

showers a child
reaching
for a starfish

Casting

Always look behind you first, Dad said. We stood on the front lawn—in my hands, the fishing rod and silver reel he gave me for my seventh birthday. *Careful not to hook anyone.* We never talked much, unless he was teaching me something—how to ride a bike, backstroke, make a kite, plant radishes. *Hold the button down and draw your pole back. Feel the weight of the sinker.* Maybe it's just easier for fathers to talk to sons about fishing. *Swing your pole overhead and release your thumb.* Or maybe he knew that teaching is good casting. *Reel it in. Try again.*

Ritual

He drags a razor down his cheek,
traces a pattern—nineteen strokes—
scrapes cream and stubble from drooping
skin, like shoveling snow off uneven

pavement. Sunk in his recliner,
he conserves movement, pauses
while sculpting chin, labors
oxygen from bedroom air.

Early 1940s, he got through teen years
in Jerome and Tule Lake, learned
to shave, smoke, and cuss.
In camp, every other word
was a swear word, he told me.

I heard him say *damn* only once.
He also quit smoking—finally
in '72 after inhaling two packs
a day for thirty years. Shaving cream,

face towel on the side table, basin
of hot water in his lap. As ritual second,
I hold the mirror, keep from saying
good enough. After ghosting a touch-up,

he exchanges Trac II for towel,
refits the cannula under his nose.
Oncologist at three, car ride
home, final look at his garden
through the kitchen screen door.

Screaming Crows

One tree
center of the garden
the pin oak you silently
trimmed and cared for
all the years we lived there.

Your tree, bronchi
infested with crows
multiplying so dense
no wind or light
could pass through. I shook

the tree without knowing
heaved you onto the bed
released the scream
of a thousand crows
a cancer in midair.

The battering of wings
tore through my earth
as your eyes swallowed mine.

Dignity lost
a Nisei gardener
slipped away in the echo
with the wind
and the light.

The Hardest Part

The fire truck siren downstairs
raided the air of my mother's dreams.
She'd scream in her sleep, my father
told me, *even after we married.*
More than a decade past

the Second World War—for him,
American concentration camps,
for her, the firebombing of Tokyo—
they moved into a San Francisco
apartment that rented to Japs,
a one-bedroom walk-up above
the Post Street fire station.

They painted their bathroom black—
It was in style then—shelved
books, unboxed a new rice cooker,
watered a shrub of Japanese maple
potted for their future garden.

When the station got a call
in the middle of the night, the rumble
of the overhead door crumbled into the wreck
that was once her home. Swirling lights
flashed ancient trees into flames
through the thin silk curtains of her eyelids.

No warning, no drill, no cover.

My father stilled her body,
his broad hand on her shoulder or hip
as they lay in the dark listening
to the slowing of her breath.

The hardest part of those nights,
he said, *was waiting—*
sometimes hours—for the truck
and the men to come back.

Moving On

The absence of his snoring
keeps her awake, the mattress
no longer tremors with every shift

of his body. Staring past the ceiling,
she melts into cracks of memories
fifty-two years deep.

Today she taps her soft-boiled egg—
a steady rhythm, like the kitchen clock,
slower and louder without the blanket

of his breathing. He hardly spoke
at meals, consumed by his thoughts,
satisfied with her way of cooking.

She stares at his chair, napkin,
fork, knife and wonders
what it might feel like to drive.

Leaving

Twelve inches off a yellow curb
in Santa Rosa, just outside the open door
of an Airport Express bus, she remains
standing—her slight frame motionless—
after telling me to sit in the first seat

three feet away. This shuttle arrived
at 6 a.m., will leave promptly at 6:15,
transport me sixty miles south to SFO,
where I'll fly to New York for grad school.

She's almost in the way as others board,
avoids my eyes—her youngest—stares down
the length of the asphalt until the door
closes. She waves at the tinted windows,

tight lips a half-smile. She tries not to think
about the once-a-year visits from now on.
The brakes hiss; the shuttle departs on time.

Artificial Flavors

In the salon chair next to Mom,
I sucked blue raspberry Icee
up a red plastic straw. Her hairdresser—

I want to say *Sandy* (fake lashes,
pink lipstick)—clucked and chattered
like a cartoon chicken. I chewed

grape shoestring licorice
uncoiled from a white paper bag,
bobbed my head to The Archies

singing through ceiling speakers
set among the fluorescent lights:
Sugar, ah honey honey . . .

I stuck my tongue at the mirror.
Its shade of purpley blue just like
the woman's hair that stank two chairs

over. Mom's hair—snips falling
to the floor like wet feathers—
was Ultra Black, colored at home
with a squeeze bottle and flimsy

see-through gloves. Eventually,
my tongue faded to pink, and she
let her hair go white under a wig
when it started falling out from chemo.

But back at the Emporium salon
in Coddingtown Mall—women
flipping through magazines

under space helmet dryers—Mom
is alive, I am eight years old,
and licorice dangles from my mouth.

Solidarity

Chewing the chicken her taste buds
forget, Mom answers the landline
kept on the kitchen table, lowers
the buzz of evening news.

Aunt Mimi, two minutes younger,
two thousand miles east, calls
for the second time today.
Kiki, moshi-moshi!

Earlier today Mimi complained
her own daughter locked her up
in a dark, *kabikusai* hotel
with only the maid to talk to.

I googled Sunrise Senior Living—
upscale on the Hudson—showed
Mom the pictures. With Japanese

words I don't know, she sighs
her comfort, hangs up, pecks
through the rest of dinner.

Before the war in Japan,
they were *furiku*—twin freaks—
clung to each other, cut school.
Now they're widowed.

Post-War Occupation

George a thin energetic
boy of 17 nearsighted
thick-rimmed glasses

operated the geisha sake
souvenir shop route
for correspondents and GIs

twin sisters Mimi and Kiki
completed Girls Junior High
closed after a visit by B-29s

an air bomb smashed the house
fortunately no one in it
things haven't gone so well

son of a well-to-do merchant
who lost it all in the panic
George was born in London

came to the States as an infant
before his father brought him
to Japan in 1937

a Brooklyn boy for 11 years
dear memories of Prospect Park
Joe's Restaurant the B.M.T.

last year of Junior High in Tokyo
his English mixed with GI profanity
but his arithmetic still good

When You're the Son

it doesn't matter if you're the youngest.
Call the hospice nurse to the house
to pronounce your father dead. Close

the bedroom door, give your mother
the privacy she needs to tell him
he left too soon. When the nurse phones

the funeral home, ask your sister to take
your mother to his garden to grieve
with the ginkgo, pine, and pin oak.

Don't let her see the dark-suited men,
the gurney, the body bag. Try not to feel
bad that your father's wearing only a diaper.

As he's wheeled out his front door, loaded
into the back of a hearse, don't think
about the neighbors watching. Keep moving.

Break down the hospital bed—the one
delivered this morning—so your mother
won't have to smell it. Finally,

forgive yourself for lifting him
into that bed, crushing his lungs,
ending him an hour sooner, maybe two.

What's Kept Alive

She crunches her walker
into the sea of pebbles
surrounding the stepping-stones,

tells me, *This bush*
with flowers is Japanese.
That one is too, but different.

I hover close behind, ready
with an outstretched arm
as if to give a blessing.

Pick that large weed
near the lantern—by the roots—
and throw it into the pail.

My father planned and planted
this garden fifty years ago—
hidden behind the fence
of their Santa Rosa tract home—

but he's gone now.
She hires a hand to rake leaves,
prune branches once a month.

Soon she'll be gone.
I'll sell the house,
return to Connecticut.

A stranger will buy it,
become caretaker of the garden,
but won't know that from their

San Francisco apartment
my father transported
the Japanese maple, cradled
in a small clay pot—

the *momiji* now guarding
the north corner—
and that my mother chided him
for bothering with a dying shrub.

Mom Deciding

I called Aaron   three months ago
I need you to come   *now*
palpitations   panic   he and Luisa
flew from Connecticut   they try
to cook   food I like   nothing
tastes right   they vacuum   dust
do the shopping   Target   Trader Joe's
G & G   drive me to St. Joseph's
Dr. This   Dr. That   Aaron left
his job   I said   *don't put me*
in a home   he reassured me
that's why   *we're here*   I tell him
I need to leave you   *something*
he said   *Mom*   *it's your money*
use it   *for medication*   but these pills
takai   cost too much   Mari calls
every day   comes when she can
two hours away   children   husband
the chemo won't   cure   only prolongs
my life   what life   I passed out
fell from my chair   now
they make me use   a walker   red
skin lesions   mark   my body

Hama

I ease a pen   into the curl of Mom's hand   ask her
to sign a check   she sits on the edge   of her bed

barely lucid   slowly forms   H   A   a faint blue
ballpoint cursive   a ripple   an echo   H   A
again   her hand can't write what comes next

her name is Japanese   for beach   I say, *It's OK*
help her lie back   wonder   as her eyes close
if her memory washes   ashore somewhere

Goat Rock   Doran Park   bright and blustery
where with bare feet   pant legs rolled up   she watches
I don't toddle   too far   into the surf

Delayed

sprawled across her bed   my mother
snores   with her eyes   open
yesterday in a mist   she wondered
about her sister   *will she be all right*
my sister   my sister's children
will they be all right   I untangle
her sheets   float them over her legs
gnarled vines   of wisteria in winter
her soul stares at me   asks why
she can't leave   she closes her eyes
no answer   for comfort
waning moons   above
rumble   of passing clouds

Memorial

Straight as steel, hands on hips,
Dad balances like a hood ornament
on Irving Wasserman's head. Irv stands

feet shoulder-width apart, arms
stretched out wide. A towel turban
cushions his scalp. On the San Francisco

Marina Green, sunbathers pay no
attention to the two college gymnasts
in tight swim trunks. The black-

and-white image is attached to an email
Irv sent this morning. He says he lost
contact after my parents married

sixty years ago, would like to reconnect.
He doesn't know he's seven years
too late. No online obit. Found me

through my website. He calls my father
remarkable—a word I never heard
used to describe him. But yes, look.

There he is. Poised in the air,
the husband who never cheated,
the father who never struck me.

Tokyo Army Hospital, 1957

She looks over her left shoulder, body slightly twisted toward the shutterbug interrupting her conversation with the doctor. *Nurse Hoshino, give us a smile!* All in white. Long-sleeved, high-collared uniform. Nurse's cap like an inverted Dixie Cup with a lacy brim. In a year, she'll return to the States, meet a guy named Joe on a tennis date. Get married in two, become a mother in three, have me in six. Sixty years later, I'll find the photo in my basement in a box, rummaging through her stuff I can't throw away. I'll post it on the Internet—*Happy Mother's Day!* She's twenty-nine, half my age. I want to go back in time, tell her something wise, or at least helpful, but having lived through a world war, she already knows more than I do.

Afternoon Infusion

She panics three *hellos*
as if startled by the noise
of an empty house,
calls from St. Joseph's:
the nurses are slow
to start her hydration.

I'm at a bar—Stevie Nicks
reverbs in my beer,
lures me back to the edge
of seventeen in this town
I left thirty years ago.

I take her call outside,
stand away from the smokers,
half-truth I'm at the mall.
She slurs a request:
milk of magnesia
and that other thing—
she can't remember.

But I remember
when I was a boy,
she told me about the mythical

Japanese custom *ubasute*:
a grown son lifts
his aged mother on his back,
delivers her to a mountain,
leaves her to die.

I'll come pick you up
after chemo, I say
and hang up, realizing
she's already cradled
by the mountain.

The waft of cigarette smoke
and hint of manure
in Santa Rosa air usher me
back into the restaurant.
The hostess smiles,
welcomes me—clueless
I have come and gone.

III. Gutter Trees

Nest

winter's blue and gold dusk   gradient
through naked windows   walls eggshelled
taupe   a chandelier-stenciled ceiling

cross-legged   we warm   the refinished
oak floor   at a makeshift   table
of boxes   sharpied *KITCHEN* and *BOOKS*

opened cartons   of pad thai and green curry
chopsticks   unevenly split   two paper
cups   screw-top   chardonnay

Five Minutes on High

Luisa stabs the taut cellophane
on a tray of frozen Palak Paneer.
Pop-pop-pop-pop, ten to twelve times
with a boning knife even though
the package says *two to three*.

I think of *Psycho*, the screeching
violins, and Luisa as Norman Bates
in maternal drag—everyone's haunted
by something. She puts our dinner
in the microwave, punches in five
minutes on HI. Over the oven's drone,

she tells me a man grabbed her
in the stairwell of her apartment building
when she was seven, clamped his hand
over her face. Unable to breathe,
she bit his finger—blood salting
her lips before her mom heard her

scream and came out the door.
The man ran but was caught weeks
later with another girl—a scalpel
in his pocket. Neighborhood dads
tried throwing him off a roof
before the cops came.

:05, :04, :03, Luisa removes
the tray before the microwave beeps.
She rips back the perforated
film, releases the steamy aroma
of spinach, turmeric, garam masala.

She can't watch Indiana Jones
drown in my video game or look
at those faceless Willow Tree
figurines in Hallmark stores.
She doesn't even like when
frozen food can't breathe.

Tripe Soup

Elena starts a joke in Spanish.
Mario interrupts, reminds her
I don't speak the language.
She doesn't believe him.

Luisa and I eat *mondongo*
with her parents in their
Forest Hills apartment.

Rubbing her knuckles, she
continues, delivers the punch line:
Tomate, tomate, tomate!
She laughs. I laugh with her.

On the train ride home, Luisa
explains the joke—*tomate*
not only means *tomato*
but also *here, drink up.* So a guy

tells his friend he got drunk
the other night with tomato.
Guess it's funnier in Spanish.

Luisa stares out the window,
says her mom's *mondongo*
isn't what it used to be. She's
been forgetting cumin and cilantro.

At the Bocelli concert in the park,
she started singing along—full
voice—before Mario shushed her.

The subway doors chime open
and close, people get off and on.
Luisa says her mom thinks

strangers have been sneaking
into the apartment. Walking around
in her clothes, stuffing them back
dirty into the wrong drawers.

At 59th Street station, Luisa and I
get up, shuffle onto the platform,
almost lose each other in the crowd.

Taste Test

Luisa surprises me from behind,
kisses a morsel to my mouth—
a gift wrapped in fingertips.

Lavender lotion conceals
the bite's aroma like the scented
envelope of a lover's letter.

I flinch, ask her what it is.
Between crunches muffled by her lips,
she whispers, *Would I feed you poison?*

On United Flight 2309

from SFO to HPN, the plane dips as we hit turbulence. Luisa and I grab each other's hand. The *fasten seatbelt* lights chime on. The guy across the aisle hovers over his snack box—a giant squirrel in a blue sweatsuit, munching and guarding pretzels, gummy bears, and Goldfish with both hands. We're all rodents in a steel tube, strapped in with little leg room, no control, on the lookout for talons. Don't know why more people aren't afraid of flying. It reminds me of the time Luisa and I first kissed, setting into motion something bigger than the two of us. For a short time after, she didn't call as often. That was fourteen years ago. The flight attendant strolls down the aisle with a white trash bag. We gather our wrappers and cocktail napkins, stuff them back into the boxes. Before we pass them to the aisle, Luisa leans into my shoulder, gives me her pack of Oreos.

marking territory

my wife stops me   in public   zips up my jacket

Riff

I pluck you like a bass guitar—
your left forearm my fretboard,
the ribs on your right side my strings.

I *boom, boom, boom* a blues pattern;
the feedback of your laughter cuts
the sound check short.

I know only one riff,
but you ask me to play it again.

Migration

Our neighbor Tray leans back on his black
Audi coupe, sweet-talks this week's girl
outside our bedroom window. I try
not to wake the curtains, reverse-peeping

through a narrow slit. My building,
a two-story row of apartments, faces
another in the complex, forming a driveway—
blacktop leading to the dumpsters.

I gave you everything, she says, half-crying,
arms crossed at her chest. *You love that thing
more than me.* His pumped arm holds her close,
hand low at her waist. In the other,

a silver-plated handgun. *Now it's my turn
to give you everything*, he says. Tray moved
in next door with another guy a few weeks ago.
Strapped an orange teddy bear—big as a kid—

to their balcony grating. Luisa and I think
they're selling drugs, go to the police station,
report our suspicion. *There's nothing we can do
without evidence*, the officer says. We moved here

a year ago from New York City after 9/11,
down the block from the hospital.
Thought we'd have a baby, start a family,
like Barb and Dave upstairs. Whenever Tray

leaves the building, he slams the door.
Damn it! My kid just went down for a nap!
Barb screams out the window. Tray
heads for his car—*Yeah, yeah.* For now,

I move our bed to the living room, the other side
of the apartment, away from stray-bullet
insomnia. From there, you can see St. Mary's
steeple, Norwalk River, and the highway.

Staircase

My staircase has thirteen steps, oak like the floors,
the handrails painted white. Sometimes the child
I never had walks down in onesie pajamas—
pink hearts, rubberized feet—counting
the thirteen steps out loud. At other times
she's a teen in a burgundy prom dress—
reasonably priced. That's her grandmother's
pink pearl necklace. As she descends in heels,
she counts, especially that last step, which blends
into the floor where the pale green rug creeps
toward the window. If daydreaming like this
you lose the count, you will find your coffee
splattered on the wall and you on the floor,
yelling *I'm OKaaay!* to an empty house.

End of October

To W.B.C.

The ground I cleared yesterday is covered
again with leaves from the red and white oaks.
I rake little by little when the lawn
is dry—better that than wait for the yard
to become ankle-deep, weighted with rain.
I wonder if it's a relief for trees
to shed their spring and summer clothes, prepare
for the long sleep unencumbered. A friend says,
the long sleep is better than the big sleep,
but I think you would disagree. I sweep
the leaves by my rosebush onto a blue tarp
not far from your bedroom window next door,
where you lay—husband, daughters, and grandkids
at your side—body fragile, crumpled, dry.

The Fern

a green glowing feather   fell from the sky
planted itself   quill down   sprouted

a body   more feathers   nested in cool earth
worms at its beak   laid eggs   hatched its young

not a flock   but a luminous glen   as we walk
we feel   their underground song   you believe

my tale   because I'm your father   and you
with the hand I hold   were never   conceived

Owl

Morning ghost—
white, burnt umber.
I heard your hoot

in my sleep. You sweep
across the road, talon
a vole at the oak's foot.

Night eyes stare back,
bronze beak tears open
the dawn. Caught

in sunrise, you dissolve
into shadow. I walk the long
driveway from the mailbox,

riffle through yesterday's
junk, open
a Lands' End catalog—

there's my mother's
white wool sweater.
She gets more mail

than I do, though
she's never lived here
and is long gone.

Seasons

midnight breeze
cools sunbaked earth
his eyes close

*

leaf shower
pages of a new book
inhaled then read

*

deer tracks in snow
my father stares at me
from the mirror

*

embrace
magnolias
bloom

Common Grace

In the rush of autumn wind, a student reads Chaucer on the banks of the Charles. Her morning desk: a sunlit bench with notebooks, blue water bottle, a Ziplock bag of Wheat Thins. An old woman with a metal cane limps to the bench, scrunching amber leaves underfoot. She liberates a surge of Ukrainian as if she never left her country: family, friends, war zones. The student collects her things to one side, stretches a tiny smile— no eye contact—returns to ninety-five pages due tomorrow. The woman continues her Slavic monologue, pulling a gray sweater from her canvas bag. Surrendering to the disruption —now an armhole struggle—the student helps the woman with gentle tugging and smoothing. An accented *Thank you*, a closed book on the bench, they exhale with the wind and watch a crew team glide across the water.

> sweeping oars
> geese float in formation
> across cyan sky

Away in Boston, Riding the Green Line

I'm not home   to mow the grass   the weeds
last impositions   of a Connecticut summer
and won't be there   before the first frost
to drag the potted fig tree   soil heavy with rain
into the garage   no raking leaves from the white
and red oaks   hickories   dogwoods   or if
there's an early snow   shoveling the long drive
salting the walkway   now she'll gather
kindling by herself   open the flue   build
the fires   and at dusk   watch the wild
turkeys flap   squawk   one by one
to roost   in the safety   of our backyard branches

The Art of Shoveling Snow

I slow-scrape the driveway
with the edge of my shovel
like I'm pushing a baby
asleep in a stroller
a frigid breeze carries

the aroma of burning hickory
from a neighbor's chimney
flings puffs of powder on me
from an overhang of red oak

small movements keep my back
uninjured and the slow tempo
maintains the sanctity of a quiet
cul-de-sac but as the sun opens

its bleary eye through a weave
of trees and sparse clouds I hear
the muted rattle of a blower
and pick up my pace

New Year's Day

Dead oak leaves refuse
to let go of their branches,
shiver in the north wind.

Mounds of moss, footprints
of spring, bleed through
melting snow. The street

like slate, erased of cars
coming or going—no hurry
to let this year go by

so quickly. Undulating past
the bare chokeberry bush,
a gray squirrel forages,

unaware of me at the window
or the red-shouldered hawk
in the sycamore across the street.

Foraging, July 2020

A black bear, size of a St. Bernard,
crosses the front yard as I sift
through a wheelbarrow full of soil.
She strolls by like a neighbor, breaking

quarantine to keep from going
insane—socially distant, amber muzzle
for a mask. I don't wave but reach
into my back pocket for my phone.

She's gone. Too late for a picture.
What's so unusual about foraging
anyway? We all do it. Search

for whatever keeps us moving—
clawing through yesterday's garbage
or picking out rocks from dirt.

If this were the day

I'd still shower, shave,
eat breakfast for the pleasure—
a toasted bagel, a schmear,
lox, red onion,
capers. Definitely
capers. An iced mocha.
I'd skip the stretching,
crunches, push-ups.
Go right to the garden,
check the milkweed
for monarchs, the yarrow
planted yesterday. Back
in the house, straighten out
my studio—just a little—
open my laptop,
start a poem,
a few lines for drama.
After emailing you
my passwords, go lie
on the sofa, text you
a heart, rest the phone
on my chest. I'd listen

to you stop singing
slightly out of tune
in the kitchen, wait
for the vibration
of your answer, drift.

humility

the pear tree   takes no credit   for its pears

Gutter Trees

Luisa and I raise the ladder
walking it up rung by rung,
prop it against the second story.
After a breath, balance it back,

heave the extension by hand—
four hands to be exact. Rung locks
click into place with each push.
The rope and pulley don't work.

In seasons of dirt and leaves
mulched into the gutter, pigweeds
have grown—or maybe hickory
seedlings—standing a foot or so
above the roof's edge.

Before moving here, we were blown
across two countries, three states,
six cities. Dug in wherever we landed.

If it weren't for the neighbors,
we'd let our gutter trees linger—
our Hanging Garden of Bloomfield,
Ninth Wonder of the World.

ACKNOWLEDGMENTS

Thank you to the editors and readers of the following publications in which these poems, some in earlier versions, were published:

Beloit Poetry Journal, Spring 2020: "The Fern"
Connecticut River Review, 2014: "Riff"
Crab Creek Review, Fall 2019: "Artificial Flavors" and "Memorial"
Crack the Spine, Issue 113, 2014: "Taxi de Toledo"
DMQ Review, Spring 2019: "Family Anthem" and "Misfortuned"
Gravel, October 2018: "Burial"
Hartford Courant, June 13, 2018: "Afternoon Infusion," "The Hardest Part" (under the previous title "The Hardest Part of Some Nights"), "The *Miss Anita*," "Watching Grass Grow," and "What's Kept Alive"
Here: a poetry journal, Issue 2, 2018: "Leaving" (under the previous title "Measuring Distance") and "Hand Tilling" (under the previous title "Tillage")
Louisiana Literature, Issue 37.2, 2021: "Owl"
Mouse Tales Press, April 2014: "Moving On" (under the previous title "Breakfast")
Mud Season Review's "The Take," March 2019: "Duende"
Naugatuck River Review, Winter/Spring 2019: "Five Minutes on High"

New Square, Volume 3, Issue 1, Fall 2020: "Ride Home"

The Night Heron Barks, Fall 2020: "*The Moon of Ubasute*"

Off the Coast, Summer 2013: "Screaming Crows"

Poet Lore, Spring/Summer 2018: "Delayed" (under the
   previous title "Detainment")

Quadra Mag, May 4, 2020: "Away in Boston, Riding the
   Green Line"

Ran Off with the Star Bassoon, 1st Session, Fall 2021:
   "Tokyo Army Hospital, 1957"

Rust + Moth, Autumn 2014: "Turning Forty-Nine"

San Pedro River Review, Spring 2014: "La Sidrería"

Stonecoast Review, Issue 11, Summer 2019: "Hama"

Thimble Literary Magazine, Fall 2021: "Autumnal Equinox"

Tule Review, April 2015: "Ritual"

upstreet, Issue 18, July 2022: "Elegy for Mrs. Mullane"

The following poems first appeared as a collection in
the chapbook *Ubasute* published by Slapering Hol Press,
2021: "*The Moon of Ubasute*," "Burial," "Hand Tilling,"
"Watching Grass Grow," "Ride Home," "The *Miss
Anita*," "Ritual," "Screaming Crows," "The Hardest
Part," "Moving On," "Leaving," "Solidarity," "Post-
War Occupation," "When You're the Son," "What's Kept
Alive," "Hama," "Delayed," "Memorial," "Owl," and
"Afternoon Infusion."

NOTES

"La Sidrería" was inspired by William Carlos Williams's poem "Fine Work with Pitch and Copper."

"Post-War Occupation" is a found poem with words taken from the article "Captain Runs Into a 'Brooklyn Boy' Running Errands for GIs in Tokyo," by Captain Pete McGovern, *Brooklyn Eagle*, Sunday, January 13, 1946.

ABOUT THE AUTHOR

Aaron Caycedo-Kimura is a writer and visual artist. His previous books include the chapbook *Ubasute*, winner of the 2020 Slapering Hol Press Chapbook Competition, and *Text, Don't Call: An Illustrated Guide to the Introverted Life*, a work of nonfiction. He holds an MFA in creative writing from Boston University, and his honors include a Robert Pinsky Global Fellowship in Poetry and a St. Botolph Club Foundation Emerging Artist Award in Literature. He lives in Bloomfield, Connecticut, with his wife, the poet Luisa Caycedo-Kimura.